TOOLS AND CRAFTS

Neil Champion

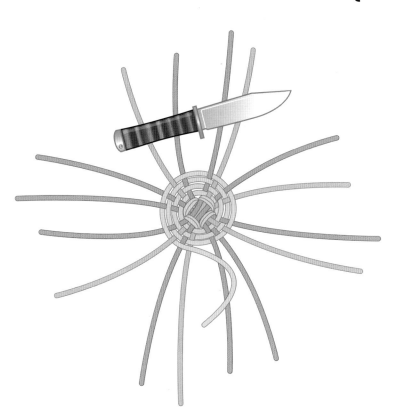

amicus

Published by Amicus
P.O. Box 1329
Mankato, MN 56002

Printed in the United States of America, at Corporate Graphics
in North Mankato, Minnesota.

Library of Congress Cataloging-in-Publication Data
Champion, Neil.
  Tools and crafts / by Neil Champion.
     p. cm. -- (Survive alive)
  Includes index.
  Summary: "Gives essential survival tips for using tools and natural
resources in the wild, including how to use wood, grass, animal sources,
and other things found in nature"--Provided by publisher.
  ISBN 978-1-60753-042-8 (library binding)
  1. Wilderness survival--Juvenile literature. 2. Survival skills--Juvenile
literature. I. Title.
  GV200.5.C437 2011
  613.6'9--dc22
                                                    2010002513

Created by Appleseed Editions, Ltd.
Designed and illustrated by Guy Callaby
Edited by Stephanie Turnbull
Picture research by Su Alexander

Contents page Peter Johnson/Corbis; 4 Jacques Jangoux/Alamy; 5
Arcticphoto/Alamy; 6 Gunter Marx/Alamy; 7 Andy Sutton/Alamy; 9
Travimage.com/Alamy; 10t Layne Kennedy/Corbis, b Specimen/Alamy;
12 David Gee 2/Alamy; 13 Peter Johnson/Corbis; 14 Angela Bellas/
Alamy; 15 Andrew McConnell/Alamy; 18 Marilyn Angel Wynn/
Nativestock Pictures/Corbis; 19 blickwinkel/Alamy; 20 Cal Thompson/
Alamy; 21 Tim Gainey/Alamy; 22 Alaska Stock LLC/Alamy; 24 Phil
Schermeister/Corbis; 25 Guy Callaby; 26 Karin Duthie/Alamy; 27 Paul
Prescott/Alamy; 29 Phil Schermeister/Corbis

Front cover: Phil Schermeister/Corbis

DAD0038
32010

9 8 7 6 5 4 3 2 1

Contents

Living in the Wild

Imagine trying to survive in the wilderness for days, weeks, or even months. Would you know how to use natural materials around you to make simple tools, utensils, shelters, and bedding? If you have good wilderness skills, you might surprise yourself at how well you can live even in very harsh environments.

*Kpelle people in Liberia live off the land, building **thatched** homes and making fishing and farming tools.*

Amazing Ancestors

In the past, people got everything they needed from the land around them. They hunted animals and gathered plants for food. They used bones, stones, and shells to create tools and weapons, and they used animal skins to make shelters and clothes. Some people, such as Australian **Aborigines**, still use natural materials in everyday life. If you want to be a wilderness expert, you need to learn their skills.

*These reindeer herders in Siberia are putting up a **chum tent** made of animal skins.*

A Good Knife

If you know how to use the land, you don't need a lot of equipment. One essential item is a good knife. Ideally, choose a knife that doesn't fold, as this is best for carving and cutting. The blade should be about 4 inches (10 cm) long. A wooden handle gives you a good grip and means that your hands won't slip, even if they are wet or sweaty.

Always keep your knife sharpened. A blunt knife can be more dangerous than a sharp knife, as it's more likely to slip when you're cutting with it.

Safety First

Whenever you're working in the wild, use common sense to avoid accidents. When using a knife, keep the blade facing away from your body. Make sure your other hand is behind the blade, so that you won't cut yourself if the knife slips.

TRUE SURVIVAL STORY

MARIE HERBERT was married to Wally Herbert, a famous English polar explorer. Wally greatly admired the way in which **Inuit** people lived off the land, so in 1971 he took Marie and their baby daughter, Kari, to live for two years in an Inuit village in Greenland. Marie was amazed at how quickly she adapted to living in a hut with no electricity or running water, in the middle of the vast, windswept, bitterly cold wilderness. She found that life as an Inuit was hard but rewarding, and soon learned many skills, including how to cook whale and walrus meat, collect ice chips for drinking water, and hang up furs to dry.

All Kinds of Wood

Wood is probably the best natural material of all. You can use it in the wilderness to make a fire, build a shelter, or craft bowls, spoons, plates, and much more. The important thing to remember is that not all wood is the same. Some types burn better, or are easier to carve, so it helps if you can identify different trees and know what their wood is like.

▲ *Whole logs can make very warm, sturdy shelters. Notches are cut into the logs so that they slot together snugly.*

Hard and Soft Woods

Trees are divided into two types: softwoods and hardwoods. Softwood trees are mostly **evergreen**, such as pine, fir, spruce, and cedar. Hardwood trees are mostly **deciduous** and include a huge number of trees, for example ash, elm, beech, birch, hazel, oak, lime, sycamore, and willow.

Which Wood?

Most softwoods are easy to carve. Many hardwoods, such as ash and oak, are difficult to shape with a knife. However, some hardwoods, such as birch, lime, hazel, and sycamore, are actually softer than softwoods, so they're ideal for making utensils. The only downside of making objects out of soft wood is that they often don't last as long as those made from harder wood.

Lime tree

Sycamore tree

Wet and Dry

Wood that is freshly cut from a live tree is called green wood and contains a lot of watery sap. If you carve green wood, it may crack badly as it dries out. If you can, it's best to use wood that has been dried out in a warm, dry, airy place. This process is called seasoning, and it can take months to do properly.

▶ *Stack logs neatly to dry them out. Make sure they're on dry ground and cover them with a* **tarpaulin** *if you have one.*

Wooden Crafts

The easiest things to make with wood are bowls, but you can also try forks, spoons, and other utensils. Remember to be very careful with sharp tools, and find an expert to help you learn before you try your skills in the wild.

Go with the Grain

Before you start work, look closely at your wood to see which way the grain goes. This is the direction in which all the wood fibers lie. It is always easiest to cut in the same direction as the grain and not against it. Some woods have a very coarse grain, while others are finer and harder to see.

Burning a Bowl

Here is a simple method of making a bowl using a thick piece of wood. A split log is ideal, as it has a rounded base.

TRUE SURVIVAL STORY

DICK GILLIAND always wanted to live in the wilderness. In the 1960s, he built a canoe from wood and canvas, tied it on his car and drove up to Alaska. There he built a log cabin in a remote area and lived in it for the next 18 years, hunting, trapping, and fishing to make a living. He also learned how to make birch bark crafts and willow furniture. Dick survived a **grizzly bear** attack and once nearly drowned in a flooded river, but never regretted his decision to live in the wild.

1. *Find a split log or split open a log yourself, using a stone wedge and a thick branch as a hammer.*

2. *Place a few **embers** from a fire on the wood and press them down. This will gradually burn a hollow into the log.*

3. *Scrape out the charred remains with a knife or stone. If you want, carve the outside of the log into a bowl shape.*

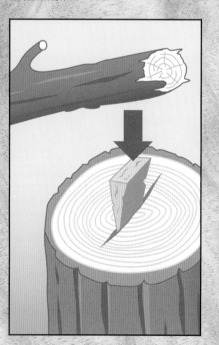

Forks and Spoons

If you're able to carve, try making spoons and forks from wood. Find a piece of wood about 8 inches (20 cm) long and 2.5 inches (6 cm) wide and draw an outline of the utensil on it.

Next, carve out the handle, then the head. Obviously a fork is harder to carve than a spoon because of the prongs! Afterward, smooth the wood using a stone, spiky leaves, or the rough stems of **horsetail rushes**.

Useful Utensils

All kinds of utensils can be made from wood, including candle holders and tongs for picking up hot food or stones when cooking over a fire. You could even try making bigger items such as **windbreaks** or cooking stands.

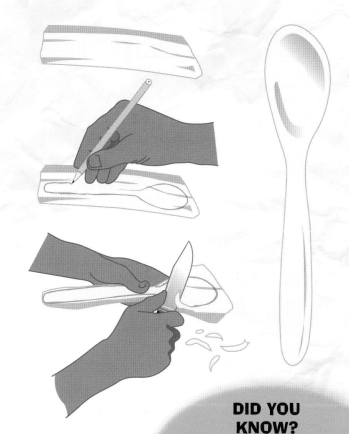

DID YOU KNOW?

Sap from spruce and pine trees makes great glue. Melt it over a fire and then mix in crushed charcoal so that the sap will set hard when it cools.

◀ *These wooden cooking utensils were carved by hand in Morocco.*

Using Bark

Tree bark is an ideal material for making all kinds of containers. Look for trees such as birch, cedar, and elm as they have good, flexible bark that is fairly easy to peel off. In the past, many American Indians built canoes out of birch bark. They stitched pieces together with tree roots.

◀ *This modern birch bark canoe has a wood frame, covered with bark pieces that are sewn together with roots.*

▼ *Bark from birch trees peels off easily. Use it to make containers, or tear it into strips to burn as fuel.*

Bark Basics

If you can avoid it, don't strip large amounts of bark from healthy trees, as this will damage them. Search for bark that is peeling off naturally, or try to find trees that have recently fallen, or look as if they're dying. Bark soon dries out and becomes too brittle to work with, so use it right away if you can. Otherwise, soak it in water and then store it in a cool, dry, shady place. Don't leave it in water, as it will rot.

Quick Cups

If you have a large piece of bark, you can fold it to create a simple cup.

1. Cut the bark into a square with a knife, then fold it to make a triangular shape.

2. Fold in the two corners.

3. Fold down the two top points.

4. Open the top to make a cup.

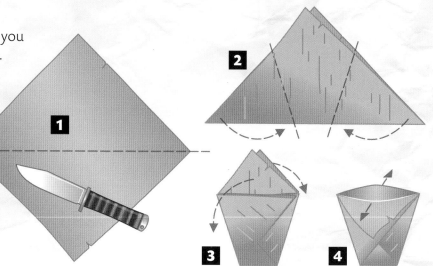

Sewn Bark Containers

If you want to make a bigger, flat-bottomed container for storing food or equipment, try this design. You need a long strip of bark.

1. Score an oval shape in the middle of the strip using a knife or sharp stone. Punch holes all around the edges of the bark.

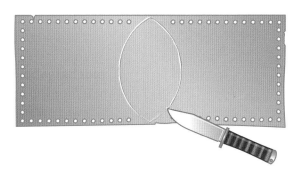

2. Bend the container into shape and stitch the sides tightly using string, thick grasses, or tough roots.

3. Use a bendy branch or plant stem to make a ring that is the same size as the container rim. Wind bark strips or grasses around the ring to strengthen it.

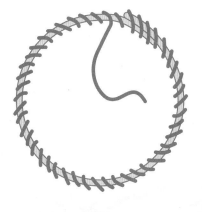

4. Sew the ring on top. This will make the container stronger, so it lasts longer.

Using Bark Strips

If you can't peel a big piece of bark, tear off long strips instead and braid them together. You could try making baskets, mats, container lids, or even a pair of bark shoes!

Branches and Grass

Bendy twigs and branches are extremely useful because you can weave all sorts of things with them. The best trees to look for are willow, birch, hazel, and cedar, as they all have smooth, flexible branches. Long, tough grasses, reeds, rushes, and vines are also good for weaving, thatching, and making bedding. Just make sure they're dry before you begin working with them, so they don't start to rot.

Woven Baskets

There are many ways to make baskets. Here is a very simple method to get you started.

1. *Make the basket ribs with eight long willow stems. Attach them together in a cross shape by cutting a slit in the middle of four stems and pushing the other four through the gaps.*

2. *Take another stem and hold the end underneath. Twist it twice around the ribs like this.*

3. *Open the ribs and weave the stem over and under each one. Make sure you pull the stem tight.*

4. *Bend the ribs up to make a basket shape. When a stem runs out, leave the end sticking out and insert a new stem, overlapping a little.*

When you've finished, go back and fill any big gaps by weaving in extra stems.

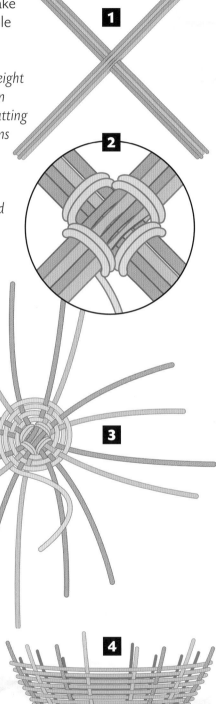

▲ *This man in Laos is weaving a large container out of dry reeds. It will be used as a chicken coop.*

DID YOU KNOW?

Seeds from black poplar trees are coated in a cotton-like fluff. You can add this fluff to bedding or use it as a dressing for cuts.

Basket Uses

Once you know how to weave a basket, you can adapt the technique to create strong containers of different shapes and sizes. Woven baskets are good for storing fruits and vegetables, as they have gaps that allow air through to keep the food fresh for longer. If you deliberately make the gaps very big, you could even use your basket as a kind of fishing net.

Great Grasses

Bunches of thick, dried grasses or reeds make a warm, watertight covering for roofs of huts. You could also try tying bunches of grass together to make thick mats to sit on, or mattresses to keep you off the cold, damp ground at night. To make a grass mattress extra soft and springy, add moss, heather, and dry leaves on top. Bundles of grasses can also make fans for hot places, or brooms to sweep your camp with.

TRUE SURVIVAL STORY

THOR HEYERDAHL was a Norwegian sailor and adventurer who was fascinated by Ancient Egyptian drawings showing boats made entirely out of bundles of reeds. Many people thought that these boats could never have been used, as they would have become waterlogged in the open sea and quickly sunk. In 1969, Heyerdahl proved everyone wrong by building his own reed boat, which stayed afloat in the Atlantic Ocean for 56 days. The next year, he made another reed boat and this time managed to sail it all the way across the Atlantic, from Morocco to Barbados. When he finished his journey, people were amazed to see that the boat was completely intact. It just shows how strong simple, natural materials can be if you know how to use them effectively.

Making Rope

Rope is an essential item for wilderness survival. You might need it to secure shelter poles, hang cooking pots over a fire, or even tie logs together to make a raft. It makes sense to take rope with you whenever you go into the wild. But if you get caught without any, don't panic—you can make your own.

▲ This woman in Madagascar is making strong, flexible rope from the thick fibers of spiky **sisal** plants.

Quick Cord

If you need thin cord or string, for example to sew up a bark container (see page 11) or make a fishing line, then the inner fibers of long tree roots or plant stalks such as nettles may do the job. You could also cut the inner bark from trees such as willow, lime, oak, and sweet chestnut into thin strips. If you have time, boil the strips for up to an hour in water with ash in it. This will make them stronger.

▶ *Look for trees that have exposed roots, like this one, and slice off a few long pieces.*

Heavy Duty Rope

If you need rope that is strong and long-lasting, you will need to twist lots of fibers together. Good plants for this include milkweed and dogbane.

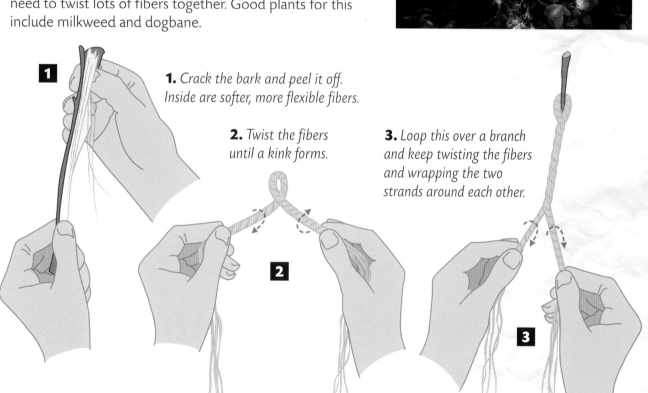

1 **1.** *Crack the bark and peel it off. Inside are softer, more flexible fibers.*

2. *Twist the fibers until a kink forms.*

2

3. *Loop this over a branch and keep twisting the fibers and wrapping the two strands around each other.*

3

Cord from Sinew

Inuit people traditionally make their own cord from animal **sinew**. First, they strip sinew from dead animals such as caribou and dry it out, then pound it with a hammer until the fibers separate. They twist the fibers tightly and use the strong cord for many things, including sewing furs, threading beads, and making bow strings.

4. *When you get near the end, twist in new fibers with the existing strands and keep wrapping them tightly together. For thicker rope, wrap more than two strands together.*

Know Your Knots

Now you know how to make rope, but would you be able to use it properly? Try to learn a few of the most useful knots to make sure you always tie your rope securely. These knots are also easy to untie later, so you can use the rope again. Here are a few useful knots to try for yourself.

The Best Basic Knot

An ordinary, overhand knot (the one you do when you tie your shoelaces) can be hard to untie once it's pulled tight. Instead, try a figure of eight knot. It's very useful when you need to keep the end of a rope in place, and unties easily. This knot is used by climbers to attach their climbing rope to a harness.

The Clove Hitch

Another useful knot is the clove hitch. You could use this to lash together posts for a windbreak, hang your food out of the reach of animals, or tie a tarpaulin to a tree to make a quick shelter.

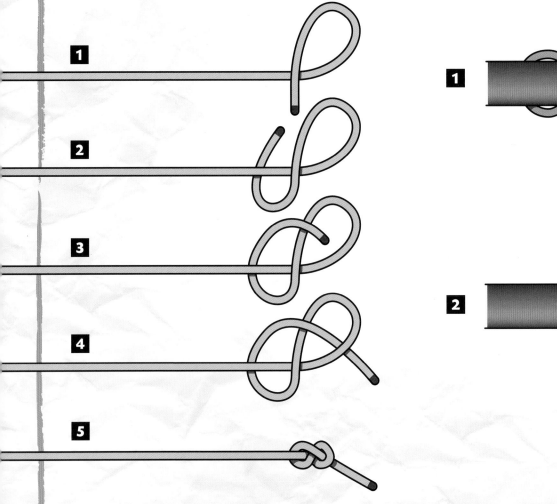

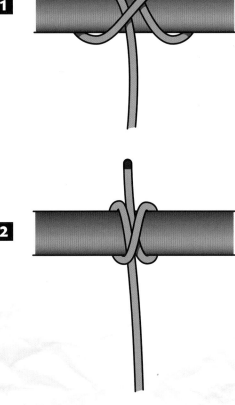

Bowline Knot

If you need a fixed loop in the end of your rope to hook over something, make it using a bowline knot. It won't slip, and is easy to untie later. It's traditionally used on sailboats, for example to fasten down the edges of sails or attach an anchor to a rope.

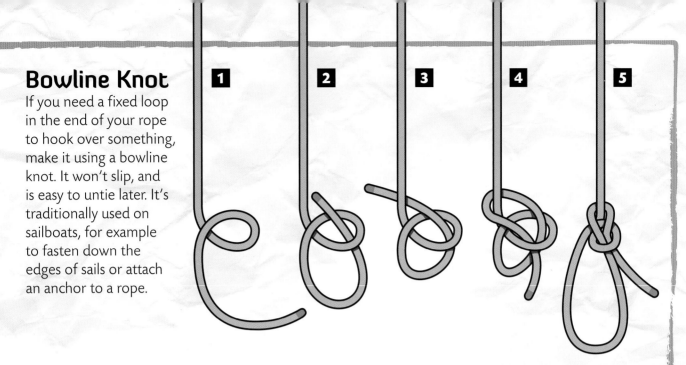

Sheet Bend

A sheet bend knot is a good way of tying two lengths of rope together, especially if one is thicker than the other.

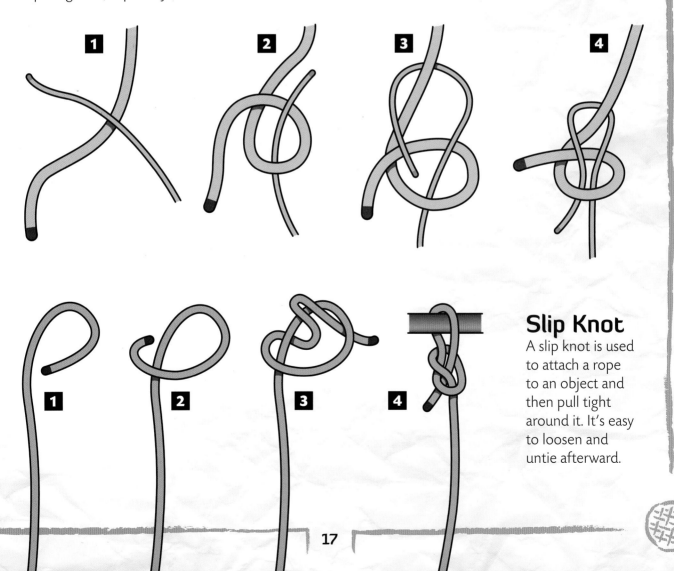

Slip Knot

A slip knot is used to attach a rope to an object and then pull tight around it. It's easy to loosen and untie afterward.

Stones, Bones, and Shells

Trees and plants aren't the only natural materials you can use to make equipment in the wild. Stones, bones, and shells are hard and sharp enough to shape into handy tools. They could be especially useful if you're in a remote place that doesn't have many trees—for example, on a vast **prairie**, in a barren desert, or by a sandy seashore.

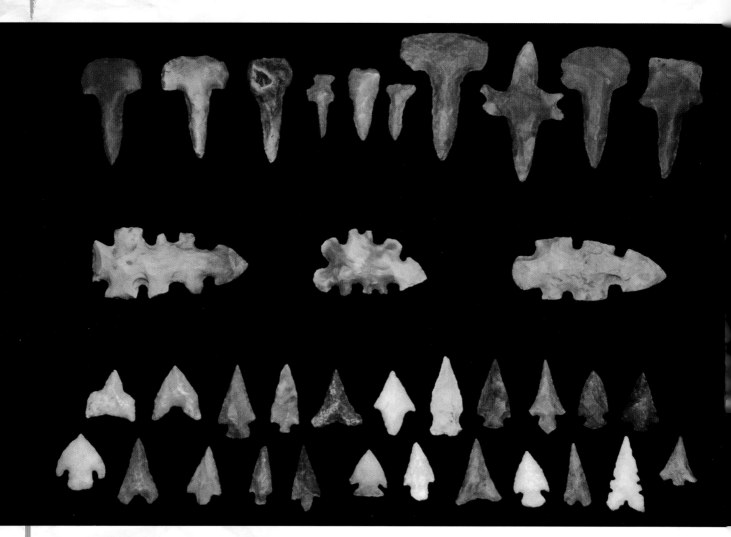

DID YOU KNOW?
To shape stones properly, you need to learn a difficult technique called knapping. You must have gloves and safety goggles to protect yourself from flying splinters of stone.

▲ *These stone tools were made by **Algonquin** Indians. They include arrowheads, spear points, and sharp **awls** to punch holes in bark.*

Using Stones

Stones are ideal for building shelter walls and windbreaks. In ancient times, people also used stone and **flint** to make simple knives, as well as heads for arrows and spears. If you're in the wilderness without a knife, you could try making a cutting tool out of stone.

1. *First, find an egg-sized, rounded pebble and steady it on a rock surface, or pack wet sand around it to keep it in place.*

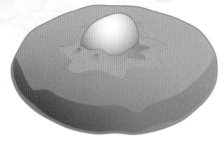

2. *Hit it as hard as you can with a bigger stone. Be very careful to keep your fingers out of the way!*

3. *If you hit it hard enough, sharp-edged flakes will break off the pebble. These can be used for cutting.*

▲ *These large camel bones in the desert could be used as makeshift spades for digging in the sand.*

Bone Tools

You may find animal bones in the wild. Once you've cleaned them, you can use them in many ways, depending on their shape. Big, long bones or antlers can make good digging and hammering tools. You can also sharpen the edges with a stone, or break them up with a big stone to create sharp splinters to use as needles or fishing hooks.

Sharp Shells

Shells are great ready-made cups, containers, and candle holders. They also have sharp edges, so you could try using them as cutting, digging, or scraping tools as well. Look for shells along beaches or try catching live crabs or mussels, then boil or bake them. This way you will have something to eat *and* useful materials to keep.

Clay Crafts

Clay is a fine-grained soil that has been used since ancient times to mold into bowls, plates, and containers, and even to make bricks for building houses. Clay is usually found on the banks of rivers or streams. The finest grains are under the surface, so get digging!

This bay in California is a great source of clay.

Getting Started

You need to prepare your clay before you can start shaping it.

1. *First, let it dry out and then crush or remove any big stones. You can also add a small amount of ground-up shell. This will help the clay keep its shape when it's molded.*

2. *Add a little water and knead the clay well to get rid of air bubbles. The clay needs to be soft, but not so wet that it sticks to your hands.*

Shaping a Bowl

The great thing about clay is that you can make whatever shape or size container you want with it. Just remember to keep the clay moist with water so that it doesn't crack.

1. *A small bowl is the easiest thing to make. Roll the clay into a ball and press in with your thumbs to make a hollow.*

2. *Widen the bowl by turning the clay, pressing and smoothing the sides with your fingers.*

3. *Leave the bowl to dry for a few days. Turn it over so that the base dries properly, too.*

DID YOU KNOW?
Some clay contains a substance called kaolin that can help soothe an upset stomach. It is sometimes used in medicines.

Heating Clay

The only problem with clay is that it soon cracks and crumbles when dry. To make your clay bowl last much longer, cover it with soil and build a fire on top. Let the fire burn as hot as possible for about three hours. When it has burned down, scrape away the soil and let the bowl cool.

▼ *Special ovens called kilns are used to heat and harden materials such as clay. This outdoor kiln is in India.*

More Clay Projects

A clay bowl with a spout makes a good oil lamp. Carefully pour hot animal fat into the bowl and prop a wick (made out of twisted plant fibers) in the spout. You can also coat food such as fish in clay and bury it in the embers of a fire. The clay protects the food from burning but allows heat to cook it. Afterwards, crack open the clay and remove the hot food.

Fishing Tools

If you're near flowing water, then you may want to try catching fish to eat. If you haven't got any fishing equipment, you can make your own rods and hooks, or even a spear. Just make sure that fishing is permitted in the river you have chosen, and don't catch more fish than you really need.

These Inuit in Alaska are fishing through a hole in the ice. They have to keep skimming ice off the hole as it forms.

Lines, Rods, and Hooks

Fishing line needs to be thin but strong enough to take the weight and force of a fish. Try using cord made from **jute** or nettle stems, or shred a cotton t-shirt into strips. Tie your line to a rod made from a flexible tree branch. For a hook, use a thorn, wire, a safety pin, or a sharpened piece of wood or bone. Make sure the hook points upward, so it will catch inside the fish's mouth.

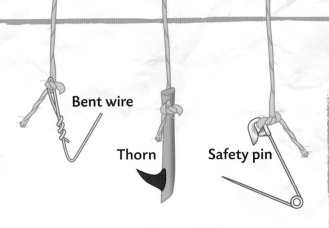

Bent wire

Thorn

Safety pin

Baiting a Hook

Look around for worms, grubs, and insects to use as bait, or lift a rotten log—it's bound to have insects underneath. If you catch small fish, you can then use them as bait for bigger fish. Dangle your line in water where you can see fish, and be patient—catching fish can take a long time!

Sharp Spears

Spearing a fish is very tricky. It's hard to judge exactly where to aim your spear in the water, and you have to act quickly. It takes a lot of practice! To make a spear, sharpen the end of a long branch or bamboo stem, or split it into several prongs.

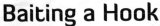

TRUE SURVIVAL STORY

ED WARDLE is a Scottish documentary maker. In 2009, he attempted to live for three months alone in the Yukon, Canada, filming himself to make a TV show. Although he loves hiking and mountaineering, he soon realized that he was lacking many essential skills to live in the wild for a long period of time. The hardest task was finding food, and Ed quickly discovered how important fish were in his diet. Every day he went fishing, but on days when he didn't catch any fish to cook, he had to eat just berries and leaves. Finally, he became so weak that he had to go home. He had survived for 50 days total.

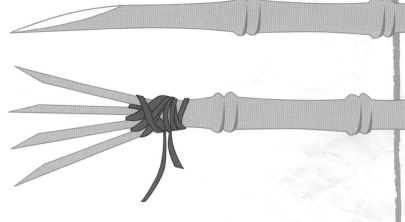

Another way of making a spear is to carve a "Y"-shaped branch to make two sharp points, then tie it to a stick.

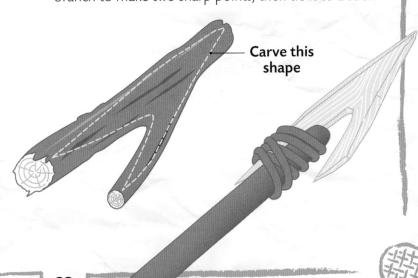

Carve this shape

Keeping Clean

If you're living in the wild for a long time, you'll probably run out of essential supplies such as soap, shampoo, and toothpaste. Fortunately, there are ways of making all these things using natural materials. Many of them are quite easy to make and will help you stay clean and healthy.

▼ *Yucca plants grow in hot, dry places. Use a sharp knife to cut the foam-producing roots.*

Soap from Plants

Soap is very useful in the wild, both for keeping yourself clean and also for washing clothes, cooking pots, and eating utensils. Some plants, such as yucca roots and acacia pods, contain a substance called saponin. When mixed with water, this produces a soapy froth.

1. *Cut a piece of yucca root, add water and pound it with a stone.*

2. *Use the lather right away, either as soap or shampoo.*

Making Soap

You can also make your own solid soap from ash, water, and animal fat.

1. *Take some wood ash from a fire that has gone out. Mix it with water.*

2. ***Strain*** *the water into another container.*

3. *Heat a pan of fat and add some of the water. You need about half as much water as fat. Boil until the water has* ***evaporated****. The gloopy mixture remaining is soap.*

Leave the mixture to set hard, then cut it into bars.

Tooth Care

You need to look after your teeth even when you're living in the wild! To make a simple toothbrush, strip the bark off a dogwood or birch shoot, then chew the ends of the fibers to separate them. You can then use them to brush your teeth. The best natural toothpaste is a small amount of sand or salt. Be sure to spit it out afterwards and rinse your mouth with clean water.

Fresh Mouthwash

The best way of keeping your mouth feeling clean and fresh is to make a mouthwash using pine needles, which are slightly **antiseptic**. Crush a handful of fresh pine needles in a bowl and add boiling water. After a few minutes, strain the water. Once it's cool, your mouthwash is ready to gargle with.

▼ *Pine needles help destroy harmful* ***bacteria****, so try adding them to homemade soap. They will make it smell nicer, too.*

TRUE SURVIVAL STORY

FRIDTJOF NANSEN was a Norwegian scientist and explorer. He and a friend spent the winter of 1895–6 in a stone hut on an ice-covered island in the Arctic Ocean. Keeping clean was a real problem, and the men longed for soap. Their clothes were heavy with grease and stuck to their skin, making it sore, and water had no effect on all the grease. They found that the only way of cleaning themselves was to scour their skin with moss and sand, or to scrape off the grease with a knife. They then used the fat as fuel.

Wilderness Sense

Whenever you take materials from the wild to make things—whether they're tools, utensils, bowls, toiletries, or any other equipment—you need to consider how it will affect the land around you. A true outdoor expert always respects the wilderness. This means thinking carefully about what you use and where you take it from.

▼ *These girls in Botswana may walk a long way to find the best sources of wood for fuel.*

Wilderness Tips

Unless it's an emergency, avoid cutting down living trees and bushes. Don't pick all the plants from one area, as this may prevent them from growing back. If you can, gather materials from several different places, so that the area around your camp isn't stripped of its natural resources. This also means that in an emergency (for example, if you were injured or ill) you would still have useful materials close at hand.

DID YOU KNOW?
*When fishing, always use bait from the local area. Putting non-native animals in the water could affect the **ecosystem**.*

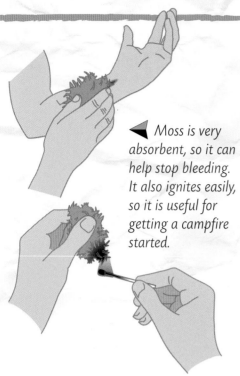

Moss is very absorbent, so it can help stop bleeding. It also ignites easily, so it is useful for getting a campfire started.

Think Before You Take

Before you set out to gather yet more materials, stop and think—could you reuse something you already have? For example, you may have used moss to make a soft mattress. But you could also use some of that moss to plug gaps in a shelter wall, or dry it for **tinder**, or even make a wick for an oil lamp. Moss also makes a good sponge, as well as a **compress** and dressing for wounds. Inuit people even pack moss into their boots as **insulation**.

Leave No Trace

When you leave an area, replace all the natural materials you can—for example, return rocks to riverbanks and sweep pine cones and vegetation back over your campsite. Anything that can't be replaced must be taken with you. Don't burn your garbage and don't leave food lying around. Even natural waste can take a long time to **decompose**. Once you've gone, it should look as if you were never there.

Do Not Disturb

When you're living off the land, never disturb the wilderness more than you have to, and be very careful not to pollute it. Try to avoid using bar soap, shampoo, or dish soap in streams, rivers, or lakes. Even **biodegradable** products can affect the environment. Dig a hole for your toilet well away from your fresh water supply, and cover the waste with soil to avoid smells.

▶ *This popular hiking route in Nepal has been spoiled by careless walkers leaving their garbage behind.*

TRUE SURVIVAL STORY

RICHARD PROENNEKE was a farmhand and mechanic from Iowa. In 1967, he went to live in Lake Clark National Park and Preserve, Alaska, and stayed there for 30 years. He was an outdoor expert who built his own log cabin and furniture using only hand tools, many of

which he also made himself. He was passionate about protecting the land around him, and reused everything he could so that he didn't create any waste. He became famous for his craftsmanship and wilderness ideals, and you can still visit his log cabin today.

Test Your Survival Skills

Do you have the survival skills and sense to live in the wild? Would you know how to turn natural materials into tools and equipment? Take this quiz and find out how much you know about wilderness crafts! The answers are on page 32.

1. Which of these woods is easiest to carve?
a) Ash   b) Lime   c) Beech   d) Oak

2. Which of these things is least likely to be made of bark?
a) A boat
b) A knife
c) A woven mat
d) Thin cord

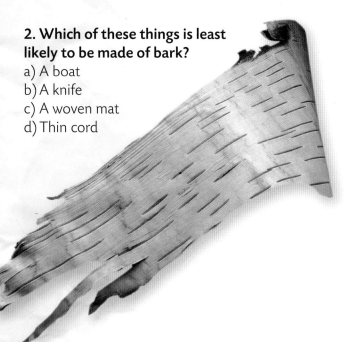

3. Which of these sentences about knife safety is wrong?
a) Always keep your knife sharp.
b) Always choose a knife with a non-slip handle.
c) Always ask an expert to teach you how to use your knife before going into the wild.
d) Always cut with the blade facing toward your body.

4. A chum tent is usually made with...
a) Grass bundles
b) Notched logs
c) Animal skins
d) Sisal rope

5. What is knapping?
a) A method of shaping stones.
b) A way of weaving reeds to make mats.
c) A difficult knotting technique.
d) A complicated style of carving.

6. Can you match each knot with its name?
a) Slip knot   b) Figure of eight knot   c) Clove hitch   d) Sheet bend

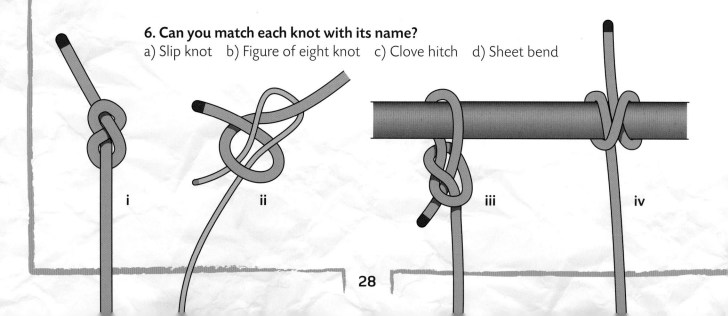

i   ii   iii   iv

7. Crushing yucca plant roots produces...
a) Fibers to weave with.
b) Flour to cook with.
c) Foam to wash with.
d) Water to drink.

8. What could you add to soap or mouthwash that would make it slightly antiseptic?
a) Pine needles
b) Ash
c) Kaolin
d) Dogwood

9. What should the hiker below do with his food scraps and waste?
a) Burn them on the campfire.
b) Take them home in his backpack.
c) Scatter them for animals to eat.
d) Throw them in a stream or river.

10. Wood that is seasoned has been ...
a) Chopped into small pieces.
b) Soaked in oil to soften it.
c) Dried so it won't crack after carving.
d) Sanded down until it's smooth.

11. Which of the following is not a good way of using shells?
a) Breaking them up to make tinder.
b) Crushing them to add to clay.
c) Cleaning them to make cups.
d) Digging or scraping with them.

12. Why should plant stems be dry for weaving?
a) They make a better-shaped basket.
b) They are easier to weave.
c) Wet stems fall apart when they bend.
d) Wet stems start to rot quickly.

Glossary

Aborigine   A member of a group of native Australian people. Aborigines lived in Australia long before Europeans arrived there, and are traditionally skilled hunters and trackers.

Algonquin   A member of a group of American Indian people, closely related to the Ojibwe. Today, Algonquin people live all over North America, although most are in the Canadian provinces of Quebec and Ontario.

antiseptic   A substance that destroys disease-causing bacteria or stops them from growing.

awl   A long, pointed spike that is used for marking wood or puncturing holes in tough materials such as bark, wood, or leather.

bacteria   Tiny, single-celled living things. Some bacteria are harmless, but others cause diseases.

biodegradable   Natural materials that can be broken down in the environment by tiny living things, such as bacteria. Many artificial materials are now made in such a way that they will eventually decompose in the environment, although this may take a long time.

chum tent   A type of portable shelter used by reindeer herders in Siberia. A chum tent consists of long, wooden poles arranged in a circle and tied together at the top, with a cover made of reindeer skins wrapped around it.

compress   A pad of material that is pressed firmly on an injured part of the body to help stop bleeding or relieve discomfort.

deciduous   Trees or shrubs that lose their leaves in winter each year.

decompose   To break down by disintegrating, rotting, or decaying.

ecosystem   All the plants, animals, and other living things that exist alongside each other in one particular area. An ecosystem can be as large as a rainforest or as small as a pond.

ember   A glowing, hot fragment of wood or coal that is left when a fire has burned down.

evaporated   Changed from a liquid or solid into a gas or vapor. When water is heated, it gradually evaporates into gas, or water vapor.

evergreen   A tree or plant that keeps its leaves all through the year.

flint   A very hard, grayish-black stone that breaks into pieces with sharp edges.

grizzly bear   A type of brown bear that usually lives in western North America. Grizzlies can be extremely aggressive if they feel threatened.

horsetail rush   A tall, rough-stemmed plant that grows in many mild, wet places throughout the world. Early settlers in North America used horsetail rushes to scour pots, pans, and floors.

Inca   A member of an ancient tribe in South America. The Inca people created a vast, wealthy empire that was eventually conquered by Spanish invaders in the 16th century.

insulation   Something that is used to prevent heat from escaping.

Inuit A member of a group of native people from Arctic regions in Canada, Greenland, Alaska, and Russia. Many Inuit still hunt and fish for food using traditional methods.

jute Strong fibers from a type of plant grown in southern Asia. The fibers can be spun into cord or rope, or woven into a coarse fabric called burlap, often used for making sacks and mats.

Ojibwe A member of one of the largest groups of Native Americans. The Ojibwe people, who are also sometimes known as the Chippewa, live all over the United States and Canada.

prairie A treeless, grassy plain found in central areas of the United States and Canada.

Sami A member of a large group of native people from northern Europe. Traditionally, Sami people made a living by fishing, hunting, and herding sheep or reindeer.

sinew A tough cord that connects a muscle to a bone in an animal's body.

sisal A plant with thick, spiny leaves that looks rather like a yucca plant. The leaves contain stiff fibers that are used for making cord or rope.

strain To pass liquid through a sieve to remove larger particles. In the wild, you can create a sieve from something made of cloth, such as a clean sock or t-shirt.

tarpaulin A heavy, waterproof sheet, often made of plastic or canvas and with small holes around the edges for attaching rope.

thatched Covered with straw, reeds, rushes, or grasses to make a thick, watertight roof.

tinder Any fine, soft, or fluffy material that catches fire easily, such as shredded paper, dry moss, or seed heads.

windbreak A protective barrier, such as a fence or wall, that blocks the wind. It's often a good idea to build windbreaks near your camp to keep it sheltered, or around your fire to prevent the wind from blowing it out.

Useful Web Sites

http://www.wilderness-survival.net/chp12.php
Find out how to build tools, weapons, and equipment if stranded in the wilderness, based on information from the U.S. Army training manual.

http://adventure.howstuffworks.com/survival/wilderness/wilderness-weapon1.htm
Learn how to make your own tools and hunting weapons while in the wilderness.

www.wildwoodsurvival.com
Read great articles about all kinds of wilderness crafts, tools and supplies.

www.wilderness-survival-skills.com
Find information and photos about making rope, using a knife, tying knots and much more.

Index

Answers to survival skills quiz (pages 28–29)

1b, 2b, 3d, 4c, 5a, 6a iii, b i, c iv, d ii, 7c, 8a, 9b, 10c, 11a, 12d